The UNSUNG HERO OF CHRISTMAS

Every year, on Christmas Eve, the elves in Santa's workshop have a competition to decide who will be...

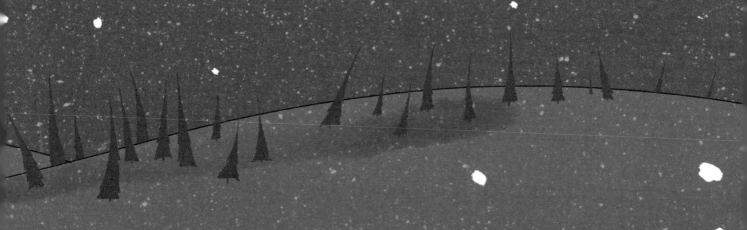

The UNSUNG HERO OF CHRISTMAS

THIS YEAR

Santa asked Billy,
the littlest elf in the
workshop, to photograph
all the other elves at work.

Santa will use Billy's
photos to help decide
who is the winner.

Billy is nervous.
He's never been very good
at anything, least of all
taking pictures.

Let's follow him and see who he photographs...

SINGALONG NICK & MARZIPAN MARK

help Santa decide which children have been

NAUGHTY

or *Nice*

Which button would you push?

PROFESSOR TOM

DESIGNS (THE) TOYS

*If only he could design
a less troublesome assistant!*

UNACCEPTABLE SEE ME!

GEL IS

DISASTROUS *Dave*

tests toys for Santa

He has just asked for a

❄ TRANSFER TO THE ❄

teddy-testing department

He thinks it might cure his

HEADACHES

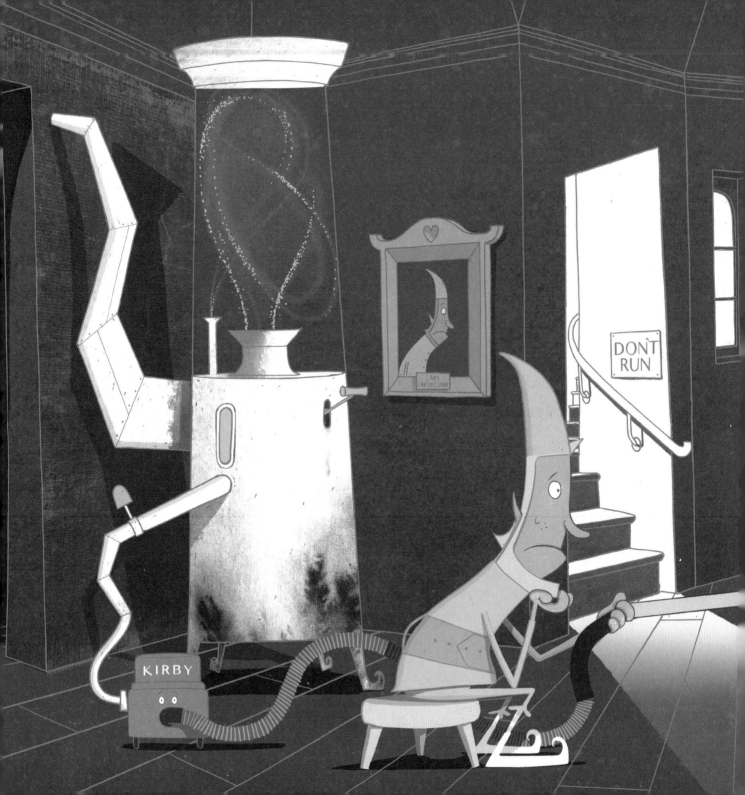

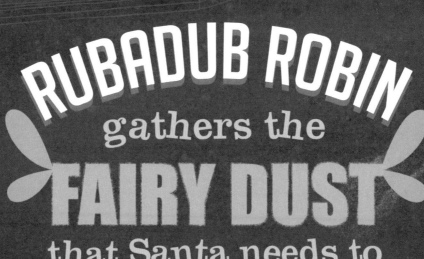

RUBADUB ROBIN
gathers the
FAIRY DUST
that Santa needs to make his sleigh fly

The fairies just think the vacuum pump tickles

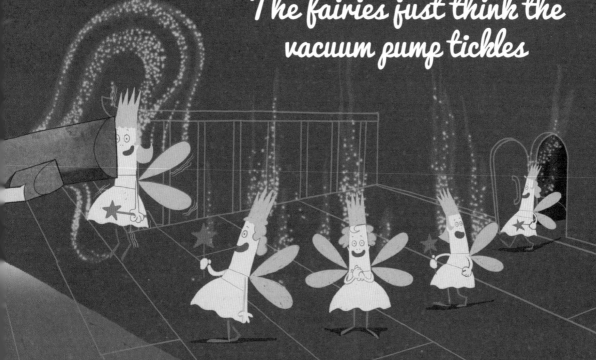

RUNABOUT Rei's

is Santa's personal

FATNESS

trainer

*How else do you think
Santa keeps in shape?*

KRIMBO KELLY & TINSEL TRUDY

WASH

Santa's pants

They have found some strange things in them:

Holly   *A Yule log*   *Gingerbread*   *Eggnog*   *A pair of roasted chestnuts*

GASMASK GRAHAM
CLEARS THE POOP

FROM THE REINDEER STABLES

He tells the other elves
he enjoys his job

He *is* lying

POOP

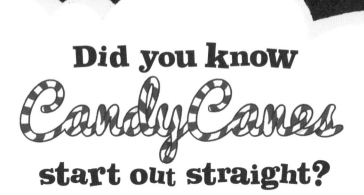

Did you know

CandyCanes

start out straight?

BIG KEV

*also turns hula sticks into hula hoops, and puts
the curves in Scalextric tracks*

PARP!

High-Vis Phil
is in charge of

ELF & SAFETY

He puts a  STOP to any bad
behaviour that
might be

**Bad for
your ELF!**

KEITH! Please don't bite my clipboard. I know its you!

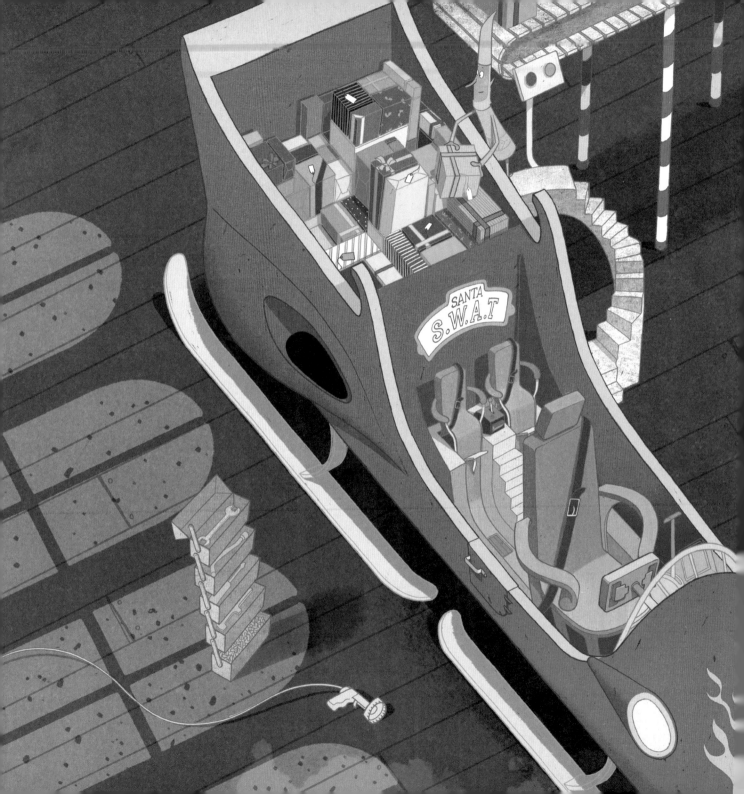

MISTLETOE MIKE

learned to pack

SANTA'S SLEIGH

by doing jigsaws

Let's hope there isn't a missing piece!

MINCE-PIE MATT

has agreed to help **Snowball** *Susie* grease the chimneys so that Santa doesn't **GET STUCK**

He is beginning to regret his **DECISION!**

LIGHT-FOOT LEE & STEALTHY STEVE

are the ninja-trained elves who make sure Santa visits your house undetected

They just love to go commando

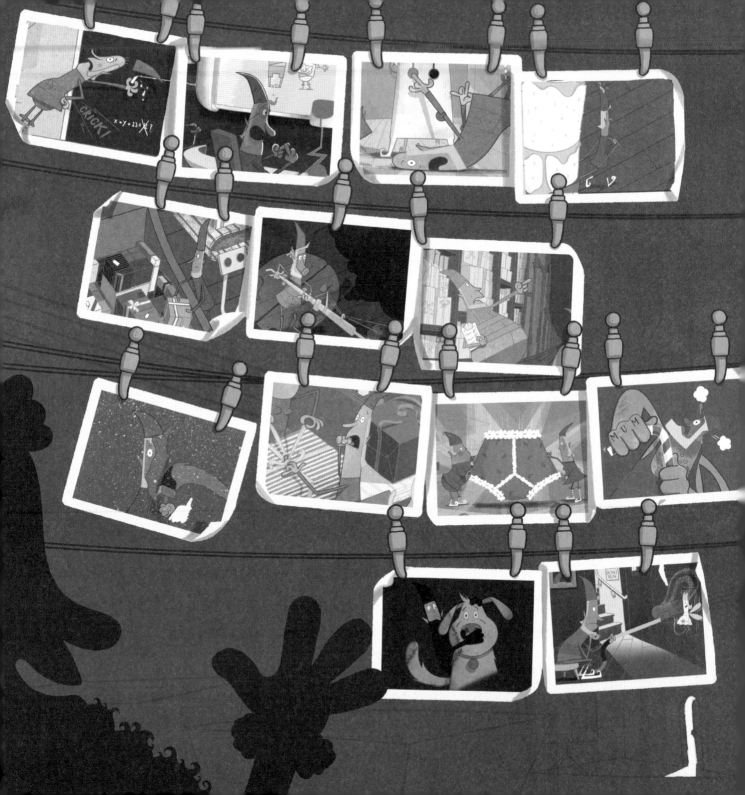

At last Billy's finished

TAKING HIS PHOTOS

of all the elves doing their

CHRISTMAS

duties for Santa

*They all wait with bated breath
while Santa peruses the pictures*

WHO WILL GET THE PRIZE?

"Ho Ho Ho!"
says Santa.

"These photos prove every
single one of you is a hero.
And the winner? Why, it's
the elf behind the camera!"

As Santa hands over
the trophy, all the elves
cheer for little Billy,
he is this year's...

UNSUNG
HERO OF
CHRISTMAS

The End

Celebrating 10 years

Juice Creative is an award-winning creative design agency based in Enderby, Leicestershire, UK.

To celebrate ten years in business, partners Nick Taylor and Mark Hodgkinson decided to undertake a project in support of local charity Rainbows Hospice for Children and Young People.

This book is the result.

"The Unsung Hero of Christmas" was written, designed and illustrated entirely by Juice's in-house creative team. We had tremendous fun creating it, and hope you enjoy the finished article. More importantly, you can rest assured that no profit whatsoever will be made from sales of this book – **100% of the proceeds will go directly to Rainbows Hospice.**

www.juice.eu.com